CW00867545

BRISTOL
RESTAURANT
GUIDE 2018

RESTAURANTS, BARS & CAFES

☆ ☆ ☆ ☆ ☆

The Most Positively
Reviewed and Recommended
Restaurants in the City

EGP
Editorial

BRISTOL RESTAURANT GUIDE 2018
Best Rated Restaurants in Bristol, England

© Walt R. Lowell, 2018
© E.G.P. Editorial, 2018

Printed in USA.

ISBN-13: 978-1545082225
ISBN-10: 1545082227

Copyright © 2018
All rights reserved.

BRISTOL RESTAURANTS 2018

The Most Recommended Restaurants in Bristol

This directory is dedicated to the Business Owners and Managers who provide the experience that the locals and tourists enjoy. Thanks you very much for all that you do and thank for being the "People Choice".

Thanks to everyone that posts their reviews online and the amazing reviews sites that make our life easier.

The places listed in this book are the most positively reviewed and recommended by locals and travelers from around the world.

Thank you for your time and enjoy the directory that is designed with locals and tourist in mind!

TOP 450
RESTAURANTS
The Most Recommended
(from #1 to #450)

#1
Bell's Diner & Bar Room
Cuisines: European
Average price: Expensive
Address: 1-3 York Road
Bristol, BS6 5QB, United Kingdom
Phone: 0117 924 0357

#2
Pieminister
Cuisines: Food, British
Average price: Modest
Address: 24 Stokes Croft
Bristol, BS1 3PR, United Kingdom
Phone: 0117 942 3322

#3
Pieminister @ St Nick's Market
Cuisines: British, Specialty Food
Average price: Inexpensive
Address: Corn Street
Bristol, BS1 1JQ, United Kingdom
Phone: 0117 302 0070

#4
The Bristol Sausage Shop
Cuisines: Meat Shop, Fast Food
Average price: Inexpensive
Address: 28-30 The Glass Arcade
Bristol, BS1, United Kingdom
Phone: 07817 478302

#5
The Apple
Cuisines: Pub, British
Average price: Inexpensive
Address: The Apple
Bristol, BS1 4SB, United Kingdom
Phone: 0117 925 3500

#6
Poco
Cuisines: Latin American, Spanish
Average price: Modest
Address: 45 Jamaica Street
Bristol, BS2 8JP, United Kingdom
Phone: 0117 923 2233

#7
Street Food
Cuisines: Thai
Average price: Modest
Address: 39 Gloucester Road
Bristol, BS7 8AD, United Kingdom
Phone: 0117 924 6786

#8
BrewDog
Cuisines: Burgers, Pub
Average price: Inexpensive
Address: 58 Baldwin Street
Bristol, BS1 1QW, United Kingdom
Phone: 0117 927 9258

#9
Lido
Cuisines: Swimming Pool, European
Average price: Exclusive
Address: Oakfield Place
Bristol, BS8 2BJ, United Kingdom
Phone: 0117 933 9530

#10
The Cowshed
Cuisines: British, Steakhouse
Average price: Expensive
Address: 44-46 Whiteladies Road
Bristol, BS8 2NH, United Kingdom
Phone: 0117 973 3550

#11
Glass Boat Restaurant
Cuisines: European
Average price: Expensive
Address: Welsh Back
Bristol, BS1 4SB, United Kingdom
Phone: 0117 929 0704

#12
Riverstation
Cuisines: British
Average price: Modest
Address: The Grove
Bristol, BS1 4RB, United Kingdom
Phone: 0117 914 4434

#13
Watershed
Cuisines: Cinema, Brasserie
Average price: Modest
Address: 1 Canons Road
Bristol, BS1 5TX, United Kingdom
Phone: 0117 927 2082

#14
Renatos
Cuisines: Pizza, Bar
Average price: Modest
Address: 33 King Street
Bristol, BS1 4EF, United Kingdom
Phone: 0117 929 7712

#15
Cedars Express
Cuisines: Middle Eastern, Fast Food, Pizza
Average price: Inexpensive
Address: 60 Park Row
Bristol, BS1 5LE, United Kingdom
Phone: 0117 925 6085

#16
Urban Tandoor
Cuisines: Indian
Average price: Modest
Address: 13 Small Street
Bristol, BS1 1DE, United Kingdom
Phone: 0117 929 9222

#17
Bravas
Cuisines: Tapas/Small Plates
Average price: Expensive
Address: 7 Cotham Hill
Bristol, BS6, United Kingdom
Phone: 0117 329 6887

#18
Zerodegrees
Cuisines: Brewery, Bar, Pizza
Average price: Modest
Address: 53 Colston Street
Bristol, BS1 5BA, United Kingdom
Phone: 0117 925 2706

#19
Clifton Sausage
Cuisines: Pub, British
Average price: Expensive
Address: 7-9 Portland Street
Bristol, BS8 4JA, United Kingdom
Phone: 0117 973 1192

#20
Hope & Anchor
Cuisines: Pub, British
Average price: Modest
Address: 38 Jacobs Wells Road
Bristol, BS8 1DR, United Kingdom
Phone: 0117 929 2987

#21
The Louisiana
Cuisines: Pub, Music Venue, British
Average price: Modest
Address: Bathurst Terrace
Bristol, BS1 6UA, United Kingdom
Phone: 0117 936 3615

#22
The Olive Shed
Cuisines: Greek, Mediterranean
Average price: Modest
Address: Floating Harbour
Bristol, BS1 4RN, United Kingdom
Phone: 0117 929 1960

#23
A Cappella
Cuisines: Pizza, Coffee & Tea, Italian
Average price: Modest
Address: 184c Wells Road
Bristol, BS4 2AL, United Kingdom
Phone: 0117 971 3377

#24
Brunels Buttery
Cuisines: Fast Food, Coffee & Tea, British
Average price: Inexpensive
Address: Wapping Wharf
Bristol, BS1 6RS, United Kingdom
Phone: 0117 929 1696

#25
Dynasty
Cuisines: Chinese
Average price: Expensive
Address: 16a St Thomas Street
Bristol, BS1 6JJ, United Kingdom
Phone: 0117 925 0888

#26
Fishers Restaurant
Cuisines: Seafood, Fish & Chips
Average price: Expensive
Address: 35 Princess Victoria St
Bristol, BS8 4BX, United Kingdom
Phone: 0117 974 7044

#27
The Bristolian
Cuisines: Coffee & Tea, Bistro
Average price: Inexpensive
Address: 2 Picton Street
Bristol, BS6 5QA, United Kingdom
Phone: 0117 919 2808

#28
Souk Kitchen
Cuisines: Middle Eastern, Mediterranean
Average price: Modest
Address: 277 North Street
Bristol, BS3 1JP, United Kingdom
Phone: 0117 966 6880

#29
Sticks & Broth
Cuisines: Ramen
Average price: Modest
Address: 48-52 Baldwin Street
Bristol, BS1 1QB, United Kingdom
Phone: 0117 925 5397

#30
Spicer + Cole
Cuisines: Cafe
Average price: Modest
Address: 1 Queen Square Avenue
Bristol, BS1 4JA, United Kingdom
Phone: 0117 922 0513

#31
Raj Pavillions
Cuisines: Indian
Average price: Modest
Address: 14 Filton Road
Bristol, BS7 0PA, United Kingdom
Phone: 0117 951 3310

#33
Source
Cuisines: Grocery, Cafe
Average price: Expensive
Address: 1-3 Exchange Aveune
Bristol, BS1 1JP, United Kingdom
Phone: 0117 927 2998

#32
Jamie's Italian
Cuisines: Italian
Average price: Modest
Address: 87/89 Park Street
Bristol, BS1 5PW, United Kingdom
Phone: 0117 370 0265

#34
Flour & Ash
Cuisines: Pizza
Average price: Modest
Address: 203B Cheltenham Road
Bristol, BS6 5QX, United Kingdom
Phone: 0117 908 3228

#35
Bordeaux Quay
Cuisines: European, Brasserie
Average price: Expensive
Address: V-Shed Canons Way
Bristol, BS1 5UH, United Kingdom
Phone: 0117 943 1200

#36
Las Iguanas
Cuisines: Mexican, Latin American
Average price: Modest
Address: 113 Whiteladies Road
Bristol, BS8 2PB, United Kingdom
Phone: 0117 973 0730

#37
Thali Cafe -Montpelier
Cuisines: Indian, Pakistani
Average price: Inexpensive
Address: 12 York Road
Bristol, BS6 5QE, United Kingdom
Phone: 0117 942 6687

#38
Chomp
Cuisines: Burgers, Steakhouse
Average price: Modest
Address: 10 St Nicholas Street
Bristol, BS1 1UQ, United Kingdom
Phone: 0117 929 3322

#39
Steak of the Art
Cuisines: Steakhouse
Average price: Expensive
Address: Cathedral Walk
Bristol, BS1 5TT, United Kingdom
Phone: 0117 929 7967

#40
Boston Tea Party
Cuisines: British, Breakfast & Brunch
Average price: Modest
Address: 75 Park Street
Bristol, BS1 5PF, United Kingdom
Phone: 0117 929 3939

#41
Tobacco Factory
Cuisines: Music Venue, Mediterranean
Average price: Modest
Address: Raleigh Road
Bristol, BS3 1TF, United Kingdom
Phone: 0117 902 0344

#42
Turtle Bay
Cuisines: Cafe
Average price: Modest
Address: 8 Broad Quay
Bristol, BS1 4DA, United Kingdom
Phone: 0117 929 0209

#43
Real Olive Co
Cuisines: Deli, Food
Average price: Inexpensive
Address: 40-43 St Nicholas Market
Bristol, BS1 1LJ, United Kingdom
Phone: 0117 909 9587

#44
Grain Barge
Cuisines: Bar, European, Music Venue
Average price: Modest
Address: Hotwells Road
Bristol, BS8 4RU, United Kingdom
Phone: 0117 929 9347

#45
San Carlo Restaurant
Cuisines: Italian, Wineries
Average price: Expensive
Address: 44 Corn Street
Bristol, BS1 1HQ, United Kingdom
Phone: 0117 922 6586

#46
Atomic Burger
Cuisines: Burgers, Fast Food
Average price: Modest
Address: 189 Gloucester Road
Bristol, BS7 8BG, United Kingdom
Phone: 0117 942 8600

#47
Hart's Bakery
Cuisines: Breakfast & Brunch, Bakery
Average price: Inexpensive
Address: Arch 35 Lower Approach Road
Bristol, BS1 6QS, United Kingdom
Phone: 0117 992 4488

#48
Maitreya Social
Cuisines: Vegetarian, Vegan, Gluten-Free
Average price: Expensive
Address: 89 St Marks Road
Bristol, BS5 6HY, United Kingdom
Phone: 0117 951 0100

#49
The Clifton
Cuisines: Pub, Gastropub
Average price: Expensive
Address: 16 Regent Street
Bristol, BS8 4HG, United Kingdom
Phone: 0117 974 1967

#50
Graze Bar and Chophouse
Cuisines: Lounge, British
Average price: Modest
Address: 63 Queen Square
Bristol, BS1 4JZ, United Kingdom
Phone: 0117 927 6706

#51
Lounge
Cuisines: British, Bar, Cafe
Average price: Modest
Address: 227-231 North Street
Bristol, BS3 1JJ, United Kingdom
Phone: 0117 963 7340

#52
Za Za Bazaar
Cuisines: Diner, Indian, Mexican
Average price: Modest
Address: Canons Road
Bristol, BS1 5TX, United Kingdom
Phone: 0117 922 0330

#53
Piccolino
Cuisines: Italian
Average price: Modest
Address: Broad Weir
Bristol, BS1 3BZ, United Kingdom
Phone: 0117 929 3255

#54
Green's Dining Room
Cuisines: British, European
Average price: Exclusive
Address: 25 Zetland Road
Bristol, BS6 7AH, United Kingdom
Phone: 0117 924 6437

#55
Kathmandu
Cuisines: Himalayan/Nepalese
Average price: Modest
Address: Colston Street
Bristol, BS1 4XE, United Kingdom
Phone: 07738 282383

#56
Lockside
Cuisines: European
Average price: Expensive
Address: Brunel Lock Road
Bristol, BS1 6XS, United Kingdom
Phone: 0117 925 5800

#57
Ganesha
Cuisines: Indian, Fast Food
Average price: Modest
Address: 54-56 Bedminster Parade
Bristol, BS3 4HS, United Kingdom
Phone: 0117 953 3990

#58
Bangkok House
Cuisines: Thai
Average price: Modest
Address: 70 Whiteladies Road
Bristol, BS8 2QA, United Kingdom
Phone: 0117 973 0409

#59
The Ox
Cuisines: British
Average price: Exclusive
Address: 43 Corn Street
Bristol, BS1 1HT, United Kingdom
Phone: 0117 922 1001

#60
The White Bear
Cuisines: Pub, British
Average price: Modest
Address: 133 St Michaels Hill
Bristol, BS2 8BS, United Kingdom
Phone: 0117 904 9054

#61
Flinty Red
Cuisines: European
Average price: Expensive
Address: 34 Cotham Hill
Bristol, BS6 6LA, United Kingdom
Phone: 0117 923 8755

#62
Planet Pizza
Cuisines: Pizza
Average price: Modest
Address: 187 Gloucester Road
Bristol, BS7 8BG, United Kingdom
Phone: 0117 944 4717

#63
Spyglass: The Brothers Burger
Cuisines: Mediterranean, Barbeque
Average price: Modest
Address: Welsh Back
Bristol, BS1 4SB, United Kingdom
Phone: 0117 927 7050

#64
Rocotillos
Cuisines: Breakfast & Brunch, American
Average price: Inexpensive
Address: 1 Queen's Row
Bristol, BS8 1EZ, United Kingdom
Phone: 0117 929 7207

#65
Severnshed Restaurant
Cuisines: British, Lounge, Burgers
Average price: Modest
Address: Severn Shed
Bristol, BS1 4RB, United Kingdom
Phone: 0117 925 1212

#66
Mark's Bread
Cuisines: Bakery, Cafe
Average price: Modest
Address: 291 North Street
Bristol, BS3 1JU, United Kingdom
Phone: 0117 953 7997

#67
The Big Chill Bar
Cuisines: Lounge, Pub, Tapas Bar
Average price: Modest
Address: 15 Small Street
Bristol, BS1 1DE, United Kingdom
Phone: 0117 930 4217

#68
Sandwich Sandwich
Cuisines: Sandwiches
Average price: Modest
Address: 21a Queens Road
Bristol, BS8 1QE, United Kingdom
Phone: 0117 925 2600

#69
The Kebab House
Cuisines: Greek, Fast Food
Average price: Inexpensive
Address: 6 St Michaels Hill
Bristol, BS2 8DT, United Kingdom
Phone: 0117 921 1958

#70
Cafe Kino
Cuisines: Vegetarian, Music Venue
Average price: Inexpensive
Address: 108 Stokes Croft
Bristol, BS1 3RU, United Kingdom
Phone: 0117 924 9200

#71
Falafel King
Cuisines: Middle Eastern, Vegetarian, Falafel
Average price: Inexpensive
Address: 6 Cotham Hill
Bristol, BS6 6LF, United Kingdom
Phone: 0117 329 4476

#72
Bill's
Cuisines: British
Average price: Modest
Address: 67-69 Queens Road
Bristol, BS8 1QL, United Kingdom
Phone: 0117 929 0035

#73
Colston Yard Bristol
Cuisines: Gastropub
Average price: Modest
Address: Colston Street
Bristol, BS1 5BD, United Kingdom
Phone: 0117 376 3232

#74
Bristol Flyer
Cuisines: Pub, British, Music Venue
Average price: Modest
Address: 96 Gloucester Road
Bristol, BS7 8BN, United Kingdom
Phone: 0117 944 1658

#75
Sergios
Cuisines: Italian
Average price: Expensive
Address: 1-3 Frogmore Street
Bristol, BS1 5NA, United Kingdom
Phone: 0117 929 1413

#76
Wagamama
Cuisines: Japanese, Asian Fusion
Average price: Modest
Address: 63-65 Queens Road
Bristol, BS8 1QL, United Kingdom
Phone: 0117 922 1188

#77
Casa Mexicana
Cuisines: Mexican
Average price: Modest
Address: 31 Zetland Rd
Bristol, BS6 7AH, United Kingdom
Phone: 0117 924 3901

#78
Al Bab Mansour
Cuisines: Moroccan
Average price: Inexpensive
Address: 23-27 Glass Arcade
Bristol, BS1 1LJ, United Kingdom
Phone: 07979 976113

#79
Coal Bar and Grill
Cuisines: European
Average price: Modest
Address: Unit SU84D
Bristol, BS1 3BX, United Kingdom
Phone: 0117 954 4624

#80
Urban Standard
Cuisines: Bar, American
Average price: Modest
Address: 35 Gloucester Road
Bristol, BS7 8AD, United Kingdom
Phone: 0117 942 4341

#81
Afendi Restaurant and Cafe
Cuisines: Middle Eastern
Average price: Modest
Address: 217 Cheltenham Road
Bristol, BS6 5QP, United Kingdom
Phone: 0117 924 8927

#82
Friska
Cuisines: Health Market, Breakfast & Brunch
Average price: Modest
Address: 32 Victoria Street
Bristol, BS1 6BX, United Kingdom
Phone: 07886 659057

#83
Halo
Cuisines: British, Bar, Venue & Event Space
Average price: Modest
Address: 141 Gloucester Road
Bristol, BS7 8BA, United Kingdom
Phone: 0117 944 2504

#84
The Stable
Cuisines: Pizza
Average price: Modest
Address: The Harbourside
Bristol, BS1 5TX, United Kingdom
Phone: 0117 927 9999

#85
Watersky
Cuisines: Chinese
Average price: Modest
Address: 1 Eastgate Oriental City
Bristol, BS5 6XY, United Kingdom
Phone: 0117 951 2888

#86
Grillstock Smokehouse
Cuisines: American
Average price: Modest
Address: 45 Triangle West
Bristol, BS8 1ES, United Kingdom
Phone: 0117 927 3200

#87
The Burger Joint
Cuisines: Burgers
Average price: Modest
Address: 83 Whiteladies Road
Bristol, BS8 2NT, United Kingdom
Phone: 0117 329 0887

#88
The Kensington Arms
Cuisines: Pub, Gastropub, British
Average price: Modest
Address: 35-37 Stanley Road
Bristol, BS6 6NP, United Kingdom
Phone: 0117 944 6444

#89
Grounded
Cuisines: British, Cafe
Average price: Modest
Address: 287 Church Road
Bristol, BS5 9HT, United Kingdom
Phone: 0117 955 5668

#90
El Rincon
Cuisines: Spanish, Tapas/Small Plates
Average price: Modest
Address: 298 North Street
Bristol, BS3 1JU, United Kingdom
Phone: 0117 939 3457

#91
Redland Tandoori
Cuisines: Indian, Pakistani
Average price: Inexpensive
Address: 20 Chandos Road
Bristol, BS6 6PF, United Kingdom
Phone: 0117 946 6388

#92
Curry House
Cuisines: Fast Food, Asian Fusion
Average price: Expensive
Address: 393 Bath Road
Bristol, BS4 3EU, United Kingdom
Phone: 0117 977 9090

#93
Hare On The Hill
Cuisines: Pub, British
Average price: Modest
Address: 41 Thomas Street North
Bristol, BS2 8LX, United Kingdom
Phone: 0117 908 1982

#94
Bauhinia
Cuisines: Asian Fusion
Average price: Modest
Address: 5 Boyces Avenue
Bristol, BS8 4AA, United Kingdom
Phone: 0117 973 3138

#95
Loch Fyne
Cuisines: Seafood
Average price: Modest
Address: Queen Charlotte Street
Bristol, BS1 4HQ, United Kingdom
Phone: 0117 930 7160

#96
Teoh's Oriental Restaurant
Cuisines: Asian Fusion, Grocery, Japanese
Average price: Inexpensive
Address: 28-34 Lower Ashley Rd
Bristol, BS2 9NP, United Kingdom
Phone: 0117 907 1191

#97
Mission Burrito
Cuisines: Mexican
Average price: Inexpensive
Address: 65 Park Street
Bristol, BS1 5JN, United Kingdom
Phone: 0117 927 3339

#98
St Werburgh's City Farm Cafe
Cuisines: Cafe
Average price: Modest
Address: Watercress Road
Bristol, BS2 9YJ, United Kingdom
Phone: 0117 942 8241

#99
Deco Lounge
Cuisines: Bar, British, Cafe
Average price: Modest
Address: 50 Cotham Hill
Bristol, BS6 6JX, United Kingdom
Phone: 0117 373 2688

#100
Clifton Village Fish Bar
Cuisines: Fish & Chips
Average price: Modest
Address: 4 Princess Victoria Street
Bristol, BS8 4BP, United Kingdom
Phone: 0117 974 1894

#101
Horts City Tavern
Cuisines: Pub, British
Average price: Modest
Address: 49 Broad Street
Bristol, BS1 2EP, United Kingdom
Phone: 0117 925 2520

#102
Cosmo
Cuisines: Chinese, Seafood, Buffet
Average price: Modest
Address: 30 Triangle W
Bristol, BS8 1ET, United Kingdom
Phone: 0117 934 0990

#103
Primrose Café and Bistro
Cuisines: British, Sandwiches, French
Average price: Modest
Address: 1 Clifton Arcade
Bristol, BS8 4AA, United Kingdom
Phone: 0117 946 6577

#104
Fishminster
Cuisines: Fish & Chips
Average price: Inexpensive
Address: 267 North Street
Bristol, BS3 1JN, United Kingdom
Phone: 0117 966 2226

#105
The Star & Dove
Cuisines: Pub, British
Average price: Modest
Address: 75-78 St Lukes Road
Bristol, BS3 4RY, United Kingdom
Phone: 0117 933 2892

#106
Thali Cafe
Cuisines: Indian, Gluten-Free, Fast Food
Average price: Modest
Address: 1 William Street
Bristol, BS3 4TU, United Kingdom
Phone: 0117 933 2955

#107
The Grace
Cuisines: Tapas/Small Plates, Pub
Average price: Modest
Address: 197 Gloucester Rd
Bristol, BS6 5, United Kingdom
Phone: 0117 924 8639

#108
Cathay Rendezvous
Cuisines: Chinese
Average price: Modest
Address: 30 King Street
Bristol, BS1 4DZ, United Kingdom
Phone: 0117 934 9345

#109
La Campagnuola
Cuisines: Italian, Pizza
Average price: Modest
Address: 9 Zetland Road
Bristol, BS6 7AG, United Kingdom
Phone: 0117 924 8102

#110
Rosemarino
Cuisines: Italian
Average price: Modest
Address: 1 York Place
Bristol, BS8 1AH, United Kingdom
Phone: 0117 973 6677

#111
HK Diner
Cuisines: Chinese
Average price: Inexpensive
Address: 58 Park Street
Bristol, BS1 5JN, United Kingdom
Phone: 0117 927 2628

#112
The Square
Cuisines: Venue & Event Space, British
Average price: Expensive
Address: 15 Berkeley Square
Bristol, BS8 1HB, United Kingdom
Phone: 0117 921 0455

#113
Hotel Du Vin & Bistro
Cuisines: Hotel, Bar, Bistro
Average price: Expensive
Address: The Sugar House
Bristol, BS1 2NU, United Kingdom
Phone: 0117 403 2979

#114
El Puerto
Cuisines: Spanish, Basque, Tapas
Average price: Expensive
Address: 57 Prince Street
Bristol, BS1 4QH, United Kingdom
Phone: 0117 925 6014

#115
Don Giovanni's Restaurant
Cuisines: Italian
Average price: Modest
Address: Temple Gate
Bristol, BS1 6PW, United Kingdom
Phone: 0117 926 0614

#116
The Lanes
Cuisines: Bowling, Dance Club, Diner
Average price: Modest
Address: 22 Nelson Street
Bristol, BS1 2LE, United Kingdom
Phone: 0117 325 1979

#117
The Mayflower Chinese Restaurant
Cuisines: Chinese
Average price: Modest
Address: 3a-5 Haymarket Walk
Bristol, BS1 3LN, United Kingdom
Phone: 0117 925 0555

#118
Bocabar
Cuisines: Pub, Pizza, Burgers
Average price: Modest
Address: Unit 3 1 Paintworks
Bristol, BS4 3EH, United Kingdom
Phone: 0117 972 8838

#119
The Wicked Lunch Co
Cuisines: Cafe
Average price: Modest
Address: 5 Saint Stephen's Street
Bristol, BS1 1EE, United Kingdom
Phone: 0117 925 4623

#120
Zizzi
Cuisines: Italian
Average price: Modest
Address: 84B Glass House Cabot Circus
Bristol, BS1 3BX, United Kingdom
Phone: 0117 929 1066

#121
Five Guys Burgers and Fries
Cuisines: Burgers, Fast Food, Sandwiches
Average price: Modest
Address: 46 Cabot Circus
Bristol, BS1 3BX, United Kingdom
Phone: 0117 925 6979

#122
Thali Cafe
Cuisines: Indian, Fast Food, Gluten-Free
Average price: Modest
Address: 64-66 St Marks Road
Bristol, BS5 6JH, United Kingdom
Phone: 0117 951 4979

#123
The Hole in the Wall
Cuisines: British, Pub
Average price: Modest
Address: 2 The Grove
Bristol, BS1 4QZ, United Kingdom
Phone: 0117 926 5967

#124
All In One Restaurant
Cuisines: British
Average price: Inexpensive
Address: 46 Park Street
Bristol, BS1 5JG, United Kingdom
Phone: 0117 926 5622

#125
Obento
Cuisines: Japanese, Sushi Bar
Average price: Modest
Address: 67 Baldwin St
Bristol, BS1 1QZ, United Kingdom
Phone: 0117 929 7392

#126
Carluccio's
Cuisines: Italian, Coffee & Tea
Average price: Modest
Address: 11 Quaker's Friars
Bristol, BS1 3BU, United Kingdom
Phone: 0117 933 8538

#127
Cosy Club
Cuisines: British, Bar, Cafe
Average price: Modest
Address: 31 Corn Street
Bristol, BS1 1HT, United Kingdom
Phone: 0117 253 0997

#128
The New Emperor Court
Cuisines: Chinese
Average price: Modest
Address: Portland Street
Bristol, BS8 4JB, United Kingdom
Phone: 0117 973 1522

#129
Jubo Raj
Cuisines: Indian
Average price: Modest
Address: 37 Cotham Hill
Bristol, BS6 6JY, United Kingdom
Phone: 0117 973 3733

#130
Grecian Kebab House
Cuisines: Fast Food
Average price: Inexpensive
Address: 2 Cromwell Road
Bristol, BS6 5AA, United Kingdom
Phone: 0117 942 3456

#131
The Love Inn
Cuisines: Bar, Burgers, Music Venue
Average price: Modest
Address: 84 Stokes Croft
Bristol, BS1 3QY, United Kingdom
Phone: 0117 923 2565

#132
Orchid Restaurant
Cuisines: Singaporean, Chinese, Thai
Average price: Modest
Address: 81 Whiteladies Road
Bristol, BS8 2NT, United Kingdom
Phone: 0117 973 2198

#133
Bagel Boy
Cuisines: Breakfast & Brunch
Average price: Inexpensive
Address: 39-41 Saint Nicholas Street
Bristol, BS1 1TP, United Kingdom
Phone: 0117 922 0417

#134
Goldbrick House
Cuisines: Cafe, Champagne Bar
Average price: Expensive
Address: 69 Park St
Bristol, BS1 5PB, United Kingdom
Phone: 0117 945 1950

#135
Nomu
Cuisines: Japanese, Cocktail Bar
Average price: Modest
Address: 81 Whiteladies Rd
Bristol, BS8 2NH, United Kingdom
Phone: 0117 973 2198

#136
Koh Thai Tapas
Cuisines: Dance Club, Thai
Average price: Modest
Address: 7-8 Triangle S
Bristol, BS8 1EY, United Kingdom
Phone: 0117 922 6699

#137
Thali Cafe
Cuisines: Indian, Fast Food, Gluten-Free
Average price: Inexpensive
Address: 1 Regent Street
Bristol, BS8 4HW, United Kingdom
Phone: 0117 974 3793

#138
The Marmalade Cafe
Cuisines: Cafe
Average price: Inexpensive
Address: 3 Worrall Rd
Bristol, BS8 2UF, United Kingdom
Phone: 0117 329 3474

#139
Bridge Café
Cuisines: European, Cafe
Average price: Modest
Address: Avon Gorge Hotel
Bristol, BS8 4LD, United Kingdom
Phone: 0117 973 8955

#140
Old India
Cuisines: Indian, Pakistani
Average price: Modest
Address: 34 St Nicholas Street
Bristol, BS1 1TG, United Kingdom
Phone: 0117 922 1136

#141
Number 10
Cuisines: Breakfast & Brunch, Bar
Average price: Modest
Address: 10 Zetland Road
Bristol, BS6 7AD, United Kingdom
Phone: 0117 924 1301

#142
Beijing Bistro
Cuisines: Chinese
Average price: Expensive
Address: 72 Park Street
Bristol, BS1 5JX, United Kingdom
Phone: 0117 373 2706

#143
Nando's
Cuisines: Portuguese, Fast Food
Average price: Modest
Address: 49 Park Street
Bristol, BS1 5NT, United Kingdom
Phone: 0117 929 9263

#144
Mud Dock Cafe
Cuisines: Cafe
Average price: Expensive
Address: 40 The Grove
Bristol, BS1 4RB, United Kingdom
Phone: 0117 934 9734

#145
Sheesh Mahal
Cuisines: Indian
Average price: Modest
Address: 13A Gloucester Road
Bristol, BS7 8AA, United Kingdom
Phone: 0117 942 2942

#146
Bristol Sweet Mart
Cuisines: Caterer, Deli, Imported Food
Average price: Modest
Address: 71 St Marks Road
Bristol, BS5 6HX, United Kingdom
Phone: 0117 951 2257

#147
Argus Fish Bar
Cuisines: Fish & Chips
Average price: Modest
Address: 114 West Street
Bristol, BS3 3LR, United Kingdom
Phone: 0117 966 4850

#148
Browns
Cuisines: Wine Bar, British, Lounge
Average price: Modest
Address: 38 Queens Road
Bristol, BS8 1RE, United Kingdom
Phone: 0117 930 4777

#149
Yoyo Burger
Cuisines: Fast Food, Burgers
Average price: Inexpensive
Address: 6 Byron Place
Bristol, BS8 1JT, United Kingdom
Phone: 0117 930 4353

#150
Grainhouse Cafe
Cuisines: Desserts, Sandwiches
Average price: Modest
Address: 14 Narrow Quay
Bristol, BS1 4QA, United Kingdom
Phone: 0117 922 1659

#151
Gourmet Burger Kitchen
Cuisines: American, Burgers
Average price: Modest
Address: 74 Park Street
Bristol, BS1 5JX, United Kingdom
Phone: 0117 316 9162

#152
Harvest
Cuisines: Deli, Health Market
Average price: Modest
Address: 11 Gloucester Road
Bristol, BS7 8AA, United Kingdom
Phone: 0117 942 5997

#153
The Social
Cuisines: Bar, British
Average price: Inexpensive
Address: 130 Cheltenham Road
Bristol, BS6 5RW, United Kingdom
Phone: 0117 924 4500

#154
Mezzaluna
Cuisines: Mediterranean
Average price: Modest
Address: 81 West St
Bristol, BS3 3NU, United Kingdom
Phone: 0117 953 2069

#155
Tiffins
Cuisines: Indian
Average price: Inexpensive
Address: 151 St Michael's Hill
Bristol, BS2 8DB, United Kingdom
Phone: 0117 973 4834

#156
Ezo
Cuisines: Turkish
Average price: Modest
Address: 6 The Promenade
Bristol, BS7 8AL, United Kingdom
Phone: 0117 944 2005

#157
The Pump House
Cuisines: Pub, British, European
Average price: Expensive
Address: Merchants Road
Bristol, BS8 4PZ, United Kingdom
Phone: 0117 927 2229

#158
Kellaway Fish Bar
Cuisines: Fish & Chips
Average price: Exclusive
Address: 4 Kellaway Avenue
Bristol, BS6 7XR, United Kingdom
Phone: 0117 944 5220

#159
Lona
Cuisines: Lebanese, Juice Bar
Average price: Modest
Address: 281-283 Gloucester Road
Bristol, BS7 8NY, United Kingdom
Phone: 0117 942 6100

#160
Boston Tea Party
Cuisines: Coffee & Tea, Sandwiches
Average price: Modest
Address: 97 Whieladies Road
Bristol, BS8 2NT, United Kingdom
Phone: 0117 317 9736

#161
Afendi Restaurant and Cafe
Cuisines: Mediterranean, Lebanese
Average price: Modest
Address: 217 Cheltenham Road
Bristol, BS6 5QP, United Kingdom
Phone: 0117 924 8927

#162
Willow Garden
Cuisines: Fast Food, Chinese
Average price: Inexpensive
Address: 283 North Street
Bristol, BS3 1JP, United Kingdom
Phone: 0117 966 3308

#163
Toto's Wine Bar & Restaurant
Cuisines: Pub, British
Average price: Modest
Address: 125 Redcliff Street
Bristol, BS1 6HU, United Kingdom
Phone: 0117 930 0231

#164
Thai Garden
Cuisines: Thai, Fast Food
Average price: Inexpensive
Address: 100 West Street
Bristol, BS3 3LR, United Kingdom
Phone: 0117 963 6113

#165
Thai Classic
Cuisines: Thai, Malaysian, Singaporean
Average price: Modest
Address: 87 Whiteladies Road
Bristol, BS8 2NT, United Kingdom
Phone: 0117 973 8930

#166
The Magnet
Cuisines: Fish & Chips, Fast Food
Average price: Inexpensive
Address: 55 Dean Lane
Bristol, BS3 1BS, United Kingdom
Phone: 0117 963 6444

#167
Steam Crane
Cuisines: Pub, Bistro, Music Venue
Average price: Modest
Address: 4-6 N Street
Bristol, BS3 1HT, United Kingdom
Phone: 0117 923 1656

#168
Rubicon Cafe and Chocolatier
Cuisines: Desserts, Cafe
Average price: Modest
Address: 26 Chandos Road
Bristol, BS6 6PF, United Kingdom
Phone: 0117 329 4408

#169
Arnolfini Cafe Bar
Cuisines: Cafe
Average price: Modest
Address: 16 Narrow Quay
Bristol, BS1 4QA, United Kingdom
Phone: 0117 917 2305

#170
Fishers
Cuisines: Fish & Chips
Average price: Inexpensive
Address: 156 Whiteladies Road
Bristol, BS8 2XZ, United Kingdom
Phone: 0117 973 8220

#171
Porto Lounge
Cuisines: Bar, British, Cafe
Average price: Modest
Address: 765 Fishponds Road
Bristol, BS16 3BS, United Kingdom
Phone: 0117 902 4567

#172
zazu's kitchen
Cuisines: Bar, British
Average price: Modest
Address: 217A Gloucester Road
Bristol, BS7 8NR, United Kingdom
Phone: 0117 944 5500

#173
Zazu's Kitchen
Cuisines: British, Coffee & Tea, European
Average price: Modest
Address: 220 North Street
Bristol, BS3 1JD, United Kingdom
Phone: 0117 963 9044

#174
Biblos
Cuisines: Coffee & Tea, Middle Eastern
Average price: Inexpensive
Address: 62a Stokes Croft
Bristol, BS1 3QU, United Kingdom
Phone: 0117 923 2737

#175
Café Amoré
Cuisines: Coffee & Tea, Sandwiches
Average price: Modest
Address: 14 Nelson Street
Bristol, BS1 2LE, United Kingdom
Phone: 0117 9976 8159

#176
No.4 Clifton Village
Cuisines: British, Venue & Event Space
Average price: Modest
Address: 4 Rodney Place
Bristol, BS8 4HY, United Kingdom
Phone: 0117 970 6869

#177
Rita's Take Away
Cuisines: Fast Food
Average price: Inexpensive
Address: 94 Stokes Croft
Bristol, BS1 3RJ, United Kingdom
Phone: 0117 924 9119

#178
Bristol Ram
Cuisines: Pub, Gastropub
Average price: Modest
Address: 32 Park Street
Bristol, BS1 5JA, United Kingdom
Phone: 0117 926 8654

#179
Three Brothers Burgers
Cuisines: Burgers
Average price: Inexpensive
Address: Welsh Back
Bristol, BS1 4SB, United Kingdom
Phone: 0117 927 7050

#180
The Royal Oak
Cuisines: Pub, European
Average price: Modest
Address: 385 Gloucester Road
Bristol, BS7 8TN, United Kingdom
Phone: 0117 989 2522

#181
The Victoria Park
Cuisines: Gastropub
Average price: Modest
Address: 66 Raymend Road
Bristol, BS3 4QW, United Kingdom
Phone: 0117 330 6043

#182
Cafe Ronak
Cuisines: Cafe Patisserie/Cake Shop
Average price: Inexpensive
Address: 169A Gloucester Rd
Bristol, BS7 8BE, United Kingdom
Phone: 0117 307 0392

#183
The Whole Baked Cafe
Cuisines: Coffee & Tea, Cafe
Average price: Inexpensive
Address: 7-10 Lawford Street
Bristol, BS2 0DH, United Kingdom
Phone: 0117 908 2266

#184
Giuseppes Italian Restaurant
Cuisines: Italian
Average price: Modest
Address: 59 Baldwin Street
Bristol, BS1 1QZ, United Kingdom
Phone: 0117 926 4869

#185
Boston Tea Party
Cuisines: Coffee & Tea, Sandwiches
Average price: Modest
Address: 293 Gloucester Road
Bristol, BS7 8PE, United Kingdom
Phone: 0117 942 4654

#186
La Tomatina
Cuisines: Lounge, Tapas Bar
Average price: Expensive
Address: 2 Park Street
Bristol, BS1 5PW, United Kingdom
Phone: 0117 302 0008

#187
Brasserie Blanc
Cuisines: Brasserie
Average price: Expensive
Address: Quaker's Friars
Bristol, BS1 3DF, United Kingdom
Phone: 0117 910 2410

#188
Simply Thai
Cuisines: Thai, Fast Food
Average price: Modest
Address: 67 Gloucester Road
Bristol, BS7 8AD, United Kingdom
Phone: 0117 924 4117

#189
Wongs
Cuisines: Chinese
Average price: Expensive
Address: 12 Denmark Street
Bristol, BS1 5DQ, United Kingdom
Phone: 0117 925 8883

#190
Bar Humbug
Cuisines: Pub, British, Lounge
Average price: Modest
Address: 89 Whiteladies Road
Bristol, BS8 2NT, United Kingdom
Phone: 0117 904 0061

#191
The River Grille
Cuisines: British
Average price: Modest
Address: Prince Street
Bristol, BS1 4QF, United Kingdom
Phone: 0117 923 0333

#192
C & T Licata & Son
Cuisines: Deli, Grocery
Average price: Modest
Address: 30-36 Picton Street
Bristol, BS6 5QA, United Kingdom
Phone: 0117 924 7725

#193
Gourmet Burger Kitchen
Cuisines: Burgers, Fast Food
Average price: Inexpensive
Address: Glass Walk
Bristol, BS1 3BQ, United Kingdom
Phone: 0117 927 9997

#194
Zen Restaurants
Cuisines: Chinese
Average price: Modest
Address: Explore Lane
Bristol, BS1 5TY, United Kingdom
Phone: 0117 920 9370

#195
La Ruca
Cuisines: Latin American, Home & Garden
Average price: Modest
Address: 89 Gloucester Road
Bristol, BS7 8AS, United Kingdom
Phone: 0117 944 6810

#196
Posh Spice
Cuisines: Indian, Pakistani
Average price: Inexpensive
Address: 9 The Mall
Bristol, BS8 4DP, United Kingdom
Phone: 0117 973 0144

#197
Pizza Palace
Cuisines: Pizza
Average price: Inexpensive
Address: 6 St Augustines Parade
Bristol, BS1 4XG, United Kingdom
Phone: 0117 929 2740

#198
Caffe Gusto
Cuisines: Coffee & Tea, Sandwiches
Average price: Modest
Address: 3 Hanover Quay
Bristol, BS1 5JE, United Kingdom
Phone: 0117 214 0665

#199
Revolution
Cuisines: Lounge, Pub, Pizza
Average price: Modest
Address: St Nicholas Street
Bristol, BS1 1UA, United Kingdom
Phone: 0117 930 4335

#200
The Brunel
Cuisines: British, Pub
Average price: Inexpensive
Address: 315 St John's Lane
Bristol, BS3 5AZ, United Kingdom
Phone: 0117 966 3339

#201
Full Court Press
Cuisines: Cafe
Average price: Inexpensive
Address: 59 Broad Street
Bristol, BS1 2EJ, United Kingdom
Phone: 07794 808552

#202
Saint Stephen's Cafe
Cuisines: Cafe
Average price: Inexpensive
Address: 21 Saint Stephens Street
Bristol, BS1 1EQ, United Kingdom
Phone: 0117 927 7977

#203
The Assilah Bistro
Cuisines: Moroccan, Halal, African
Average price: Modest
Address: 194 -196 Wells Road
Bristol, BS4 2, United Kingdom
Phone: 07816 202827

#204
Spitfire
Cuisines: Barbeque
Average price: Modest
Address: 1 Hannover Quay
Bristol, BS1 5JE, United Kingdom
Phone: 0117 925 4585

#205
Bella Italia
Cuisines: Italian
Average price: Inexpensive
Address: Unit SU57
Bristol, BS1 3BX, United Kingdom
Phone: 0117 927 7230

#206
Havana Coffee
Cuisines: Coffee & Tea, Breakfast & Brunch
Average price: Inexpensive
Address: 37A Cotham Hill
Bristol, BS6 6JY, United Kingdom
Phone: 0117 973 3020

#207
Cote Brasserie
Cuisines: French, Mediterranean, British
Average price: Expensive
Address: 27 The Mall
Bristol, BS8 4JG, United Kingdom
Phone: 0117 970 6779

#208
My Burrito
Cuisines: Mexican
Average price: Inexpensive
Address: 7 Broad Quay
Bristol, BS1 4DA, United Kingdom
Phone: 0117 929 7239

#209
Headley Fish Bar
Cuisines: Fish & Chips
Average price: Inexpensive
Address: A 1 ST. Peters Rise
Bristol, BS13 7LU, United Kingdom
Phone: 0117 964 0698

#210
Zizzi
Cuisines: Italian
Average price: Modest
Address: 29 Princess Victoria Street
Bristol, BS8 4BX, United Kingdom
Phone: 0117 317 9842

#211
La Tasca
Cuisines: Tapas Bar, Spanish
Average price: Expensive
Address: The Glass House
Bristol, BS1 3BX, United Kingdom
Phone: 0845 129 7623

#212
Strada
Cuisines: Italian
Average price: Modest
Address: 34 Princess Victoria Street
Bristol, BS8 4BZ, United Kingdom
Phone: 0117 923 7224

#213
Magic Roll
Cuisines: British
Average price: Inexpensive
Address: Redcliff St
Bristol, BS1 6JG, United Kingdom
Phone: 07851 760939

#214
Las Iguanas
Cuisines: Cuban, Cocktail Bar
Average price: Modest
Address: Anchor Square
Bristol, BS1 5UH, United Kingdom
Phone: 0117 927 6233

#215
Tasty Stop
Cuisines: Diner
Average price: Inexpensive
Address: 202 North St
Bristol, BS3 1JF, United Kingdom
Phone: 0117 953 7648

#216
The Townhouse Bar & Restaurant
Cuisines: European, British, Pub
Average price: Expensive
Address: 85 Whiteladies Road
Bristol, BS8 2NT, United Kingdom
Phone: 0117 973 9302

#217
Nando's
Cuisines: Portuguese
Average price: Modest
Address: Lysander Road
Bristol, BS34 5UL, United Kingdom
Phone: 0117 959 0146

#218
Wagamama Bristol
Cuisines: Japanese
Average price: Modest
Address: Glass House
Bristol, BS2 0HH, United Kingdom
Phone: 0117 927 7674

#219
The Kitchen
Cuisines: Cafe Burgers
Average price: Inexpensive
Address: Silver Street
Bristol, BS1 2AG, United Kingdom
Phone: 0117 929 2975

#220
The Olive Shed Shop
Cuisines: Deli, Greek, Specialty Food
Average price: Modest
Address: 123 Gloucester Road
Bristol, BS7 8AX, United Kingdom
Phone: 0117 924 0572

#221
Chin! Chin! Bar & Kitchen
Cuisines: Wine Bar, British, Pub
Average price: Modest
Address: 155 Saint Michael's Hill
Bristol, BS2 8DB, United Kingdom
Phone: 0117 973 9393

#222
The Shakespeare
Cuisines: Pub, British
Average price: Modest
Address: Lower Redland Road
Bristol, BS6 6SS, United Kingdom
Phone: 0117 973 9850

#223
Bottelino's
Cuisines: Italian
Average price: Modest
Address: The Old Police Station
Bristol, BS3 4HS, United Kingdom
Phone: 0117 966 6676

#224
Aqua Bar & Restaurant
Cuisines: Italian, Pizza
Average price: Expensive
Address: 153 Whiteladies Rd
Bristol, BS8 2RF, United Kingdom
Phone: 0117 973 3314

#225
Ahmed's Curry Cafe
Cuisines: Indian, Pakistani
Average price: Inexpensive
Address: 1e Chandos Road
Bristol, BS6 6PG, United Kingdom
Phone: 0117 946 6466

#226
China Capital
Cuisines: Fast Food, Chinese
Average price: Modest
Address: 10 Gloucester Road N
Bristol, BS7 0SF, United Kingdom
Phone: 0117 969 5486

#227
Pret a Manger
Cuisines: Coffee & Tea, Sandwiches
Average price: Inexpensive
Address: Glass Walk
Bristol, BS1 3BD, United Kingdom
Phone: 020 7932 5396

#228
Joy Raj Indian Restaurant
Cuisines: Indian
Average price: Modest
Address: 31 Regent Street
Bristol, BS8 4HR, United Kingdom
Phone: 0117 973 8101

#229
Cafe A Roma
Cuisines: Coffee & Tea, Italian, Tea Room
Average price: Inexpensive
Address: 234 Cheltenham Road
Bristol, BS6 5QU, United Kingdom
Phone: 0117 904 7302

#230
Marhaba Bistro
Cuisines: Moroccan
Average price: Modest
Address: 611 Fishponds Road
Bristol, BS16 3AA, United Kingdom
Phone: 0117 965 0752

#231
Arch House Deli
Cuisines: Deli, Cafe, Cheese Shop
Average price: Modest
Address: Boyces Avenue
Bristol, BS8 4AA, United Kingdom
Phone: 0117 974 1166

#232
Greenhouse
Cuisines: Pub, British
Average price: Inexpensive
Address: 37 College Green
Bristol, BS1 5SP, United Kingdom
Phone: 0117 927 6426

#233
Wahaca
Cuisines: Mexican
Average price: Modest
Address: 70-78 Queens Road
Bristol, BS8 1QU, United Kingdom
Phone: 0117 332 4486

#234
Pizza Express
Cuisines: Pizza, Italian
Average price: Expensive
Address: 31 Berkeley Square
Bristol, BS8 1HP, United Kingdom
Phone: 0117 926 0300

#235
Pepenero
Cuisines: Pizza, Italian, Vegan
Average price: Modest
Address: 22 Bond Street
Bristol, BS2 3LU, United Kingdom
Phone: 0117 926 8057

#236
The Bristologist
Cuisines: Bar, British
Average price: Modest
Address: 47 Corn Street
Bristol, BS1 1HT, United Kingdom
Phone: 0117 930 4762

#237
The Curry Centre
Cuisines: Fast Food
Average price: Inexpensive
Address: 43 West Street
Bristol, BS3 3NS, United Kingdom
Phone: 0117 953 2637

#238
The Anchor
Cuisines: Pub, British
Average price: Inexpensive
Address: 323 Gloucester Road
Bristol, BS7 8PE, United Kingdom
Phone: 0117 924 1769

#239
Toby Carvery
Cuisines: Pub, British
Average price: Modest
Address: 189 Henbury Road
Bristol, BS10 7AD, United Kingdom
Phone: 0117 950 0144

#240
Yo! Sushi
Cuisines: Sushi Bar
Average price: Modest
Address: Glass Walk
Bristol, BS1 3BQ, United Kingdom
Phone: 0117 321 3161

#241
Peckish
Cuisines: Breakfast & Brunch, Sandwiches
Average price: Inexpensive
Address: 61 Union Street
Bristol, BS1, United Kingdom
Phone: 0117 929 8588

#242
Yum Yum Thai
Cuisines: Thai, Asian Fusion
Average price: Modest
Address: 50 Park St
Bristol, BS1 5JN, United Kingdom
Phone: 0117 929 0987

#243
Coronation Curry House
Cuisines: Indian
Average price: Modest
Address: 190 Coronation Road
Bristol, BS3 1RF, United Kingdom
Phone: 0117 966 4569

#244
No Man's Grace
Cuisines: Tapas/Small Plates, Wine Bar
Average price: Modest
Address: 6 Chandos Road
Bristol, BS6 6PE, United Kingdom
Phone: 0117 974 4077

#245
Bombay Spice
Cuisines: Indian, Pakistani
Average price: Exclusive
Address: 10 The Mall
Bristol, BS8 4DR, United Kingdom
Phone: 0117 970 6066

#246
Fresh Takeaway
Cuisines: Fast Food, Chinese
Average price: Modest
Address: 124 St Michael's Hill
Bristol, BS2 8BU, United Kingdom
Phone: 0117 926 5959

#247
Chandos Deli
Cuisines: Deli
Average price: Modest
Address: 121 Whiteladies Road
Bristol, BS8 2PL, United Kingdom
Phone: 0117 970 6565

#248
Mocha Mocha
Cuisines: Coffee & Tea, Sandwiches
Average price: Modest
Address: 139 St Michaels Hill
Bristol, BS2 8BS, United Kingdom
Phone: 0117 929 8880

#249
Mange Tout
Cuisines: Fast Food, Coffee & Tea
Average price: Inexpensive
Address: 58 Corn Street
Bristol, BS1 1JG, United Kingdom
Phone: 0117 927 7927

#250
Old Market Tavern
Cuisines: Pub, British
Average price: Inexpensive
Address: 29-30 Old Market Street
Bristol, BS2 0HB, United Kingdom
Phone: 0117 922 6123

#251
Pizza Provencale
Cuisines: Pizza, French, Gluten-Free
Average price: Modest
Address: 29 Regent Street
Bristol, BS8 4HR, United Kingdom
Phone: 0117 974 1175

#252
Cordial & Grace
Cuisines: Cafe
Average price: Modest
Address: 9 The Mall
Bristol, BS8 4DP, United Kingdom
Phone: 0117 970 6259

#253
Subway
Cuisines: Sandwiches
Average price: Inexpensive
Address: 9 Clare Street
Bristol, BS1 1XH, United Kingdom
Phone: 0117 930 0455

#254
Savana Coffee
Cuisines: Coffee & Tea, Mediterranean
Average price: Modest
Address: 273 North Street
Bristol, BS3 1JN, United Kingdom
Phone: 0117 966 0088

#255
Piazza Di Roma
Cuisines: Pizza
Average price: Modest
Address: 178 Whiteladies Road
Bristol, BS8 2XU, United Kingdom
Phone: 0117 973 4183

#256
Jolly Fryer
Cuisines: Fish & Chips, Burgers
Average price: Inexpensive
Address: 557A Filton Avenue
Bristol, BS7 0QH, United Kingdom
Phone: 0117 969 2376

#257
Boulangerie
Cuisines: Bakery, Coffee & Tea, Sandwiches
Average price: Inexpensive
Address: 3 Queens Rd
Bristol, BS8 1QE, United Kingdom
Phone: 0117 929 3983

#258
Brigstow Cafe & Tapas
Cuisines: British, Coffee & Tea, Tapas
Average price: Modest
Address: 9 Clare Street
Bristol, BS1 1XH, United Kingdom
Phone: 0117 929 3876

#259
Bristol Fryer
Cuisines: Fish & Chips, Coffee & Tea
Average price: Inexpensive
Address: 431 Gloucester Road
Bristol, BS7 8TZ, United Kingdom
Phone: 0117 951 5415

#260
New Ki Lee Fish Bar
Cuisines: Fish & Chips, Chinese, Fast Food
Average price: Modest
Address: 90 Mina Road
Bristol, BS2 9XW, United Kingdom
Phone: 0117 955 1044

#261
John's York Cafe
Cuisines: Breakfast & Brunch, British
Average price: Inexpensive
Address: 46 Bond St
Bristol, BS1, United Kingdom
Phone: 0117 929 0101

#262
The Lazy Dog
Cuisines: British, Gastropub
Average price: Modest
Address: 112 Ashley Down Road
Bristol, BS7 9JR, United Kingdom
Phone: 0117 924 4809

#263
Masa Japanese Restaurant
Cuisines: Japanese
Average price: Modest
Address: 42-46 Baldwin St
Bristol, BS1 1PN, United Kingdom
Phone: 0117 929 3888

#264
Giraffe
Cuisines: American
Average price: Modest
Address: Glass House
Bristol, BS2 9AB, United Kingdom
Phone: 0117 930 0603

#265
Cafe Du Jour
Cuisines: Coffee & Tea, French
Average price: Inexpensive
Address: 72 Whiteladies Road
Bristol, BS8 2QA, United Kingdom
Phone: 0117 973 1563

#266
The Scotchman & His Pack
Cuisines: Pub, British
Average price: Modest
Address: 20 St Michaels Hill
Bristol, BS2 8DX, United Kingdom
Phone: 0117 373 0138

#267
Basmati
Cuisines: Cafe
Average price: Modest
Address: 114 Rodway Road
Bristol, BS34 5PG, United Kingdom
Phone: 0117 969 9777

#268
Woodes Cafe
Cuisines: Coffee & Tea, Sandwiches
Average price: Inexpensive
Address: 18 Park Street
Bristol, BS1 5JA, United Kingdom
Phone: 0117 926 4041

#269
O'Neill's
Cuisines: Irish, Bar
Average price: Inexpensive
Address: 16-24 Baldwin Street
Bristol, BS1 1SE, United Kingdom
Phone: 0117 945 8891

#270
Nazar Meze Restaurant
Cuisines: Mediterranean, Turkish
Average price: Modest
Address: 599 Fishponds Road
Bristol, BS16 3AA, United Kingdom
Phone: 0117 378 9379

#271
Lal Jomi Pavillion Restaurant
Cuisines: Indian, Pakistani
Average price: Modest
Address: 2 Harcourt Road
Bristol, BS6 7RG, United Kingdom
Phone: 0117 942 1640

#272
Thai Pepper
Cuisines: Fast Food, Thai
Average price: Modest
Address: 215 Cheltenham Road
Bristol, BS6 5QP, United Kingdom
Phone: 0117 924 9402

#273
The Walrus & Carpenter
Cuisines: British
Average price: Modest
Address: 1 Regent Street
Bristol, BS8 4HW, United Kingdom
Phone: 0117 974 3793

#274
Yia Mass
Cuisines: Bar, Mediterranean
Average price: Expensive
Address: 67 Park Street
Bristol, BS1 5PB, United Kingdom
Phone: 0117 929 9530

#275
Brace & Browns
Cuisines: Tapas Bar
Average price: Expensive
Address: 43 Whiteladies Road
Bristol, BS5 2LS, United Kingdom
Phone: 0117 973 7800

#276
River Cottage Canteen
Cuisines: British
Average price: Expensive
Address: St John's Court
Bristol, BS8 2QY, United Kingdom
Phone: 0117 973 2458

#277
Sandwich Sandwich
Cuisines: Sandwiches, Cafe
Average price: Inexpensive
Address: 52 Baldwin Street
Bristol, BS1 1QQ, United Kingdom
Phone: 0117 929 2330

#278
Chandos Delicatessen
Cuisines: Deli, Food
Average price: Expensive
Address: 6 Princess Victoria Street
Bristol, BS8 4BP, United Kingdom
Phone: 0117 974 3275

#279
Siam Harbourside Thai Restaurant
Cuisines: Thai
Average price: Expensive
Address: 129 Hotwell Rd
Bristol, BS8 4RU, United Kingdom
Phone: 0117 330 6476

#280
Di Meo
Cuisines: Italian
Average price: Modest
Address: 314 Gloucester Road
Bristol, BS7 8, United Kingdom
Phone: 0117 924 5676

#281
The Hawthorns
Cuisines: Hotel, Breakfast & Brunch
Average price: Inexpensive
Address: Woodland Road
Bristol, BS8 1UQ, United Kingdom
Phone: 0117 954 6638

#282
Best Spice
Cuisines: Indian, Fast Food
Average price: Inexpensive
Address: 180 Wells Road
Bristol, BS4 2AL, United Kingdom
Phone: 0117 971 7758

#283
The White Harte
Cuisines: Pub, British, Pool Halls
Average price: Inexpensive
Address: 54-58 Park Row
Bristol, BS1 5LH, United Kingdom
Phone: 0117 929 2490

#284
The Knights Templar
Cuisines: British, Pub
Average price: Inexpensive
Address: 1 The Square
Bristol, BS1 6DG, United Kingdom
Phone: 0117 930 8710

#285
Kalahari Moon
Cuisines: Deli, Grocery, Beer, Wine & Spirits
Average price: Modest
Address: 88-91 The Covered Market
Bristol, BS1 1JQ, United Kingdom
Phone: 0117 929 9879

#286
Gert Lush
Cuisines: Sandwiches
Average price: Inexpensive
Address: 9A Regent Street
Bristol, BS8 4HW, United Kingdom
Phone: 0117 973 1003

#287
Q.E.D. Bistro
Cuisines: Sandwiches
Average price: Inexpensive
Address: 122 St Michael's Hill
Bristol, BS2 8BU, United Kingdom
Phone: 0117 929 3803

#288
Rummer Hotel
Cuisines: British, Cocktail Bar
Average price: Expensive
Address: All Saints Lane
Bristol, BS1 1JH, United Kingdom
Phone: 0117 929 0111

#289
Thai Basil Restaurant
Cuisines: Thai
Average price: Expensive
Address: 28 High Street
Bristol, BS35 2AH, United Kingdom
Phone: 01454 418122

#290
The Clifton Wine Bar
Cuisines: British, Pub, Beer Gardens
Average price: Modest
Address: 3-5 Richmond Terrace
Bristol, BS8 1AB, United Kingdom
Phone: 0117 973 7866

#291
Shore Cafe Bar
Cuisines: Burgers, Pub
Average price: Modest
Address: Prince Street
Bristol, BS1 4QF, United Kingdom
Phone: 0117 923 0333

#292
Vincenzo's Pizza House
Cuisines: Pizza, Italian
Average price: Inexpensive
Address: 71a Park Street
Bristol, BS1 5PB, United Kingdom
Phone: 0117 926 0908

#293
Asian Spicy
Cuisines: Fast Food, Indian, Pakistani
Average price: Modest
Address: 202 Cheltenham Road
Bristol, BS6 5QZ, United Kingdom
Phone: 0117 924 3701

#294
Aquila
Cuisines: Italian, Wine Bar
Average price: Modest
Address: 30/34 Baldwin Street
Bristol, BS1, United Kingdom
Phone: 0117 321 0322

#295
Al Bacio Italian Restaurant
Cuisines: Italian
Average price: Modest
Address: 95 Queens Road
Bristol, BS8 1LW, United Kingdom
Phone: 0117 973 9734

#296
Domino's
Cuisines: Pizza
Average price: Modest
Address: 119 Whiteladies Road
Bristol, BS8 2PL, United Kingdom
Phone: 0117 973 3400

#297
Pizza Express
Cuisines: Pizza, Italian
Average price: Modest
Address: Unit 1 Building 8
Bristol, BS1 5TY, United Kingdom
Phone: 0117 927 3622

#298
Monte Carlo Cafe
Cuisines: Breakfast & Brunch
Average price: Inexpensive
Address: 458 Stapleton Road
Bristol, BS5 6, United Kingdom
Phone: 0117 951 0199

#299
Willow Curry Bar
Cuisines: Fast Food
Average price: Inexpensive
Address: 86 St Johns Ln
Bristol, BS3 5AQ, United Kingdom
Phone: 0117 977 8910

#300
Undercroft Cafe
Cuisines: Coffee & Tea, British
Average price: Inexpensive
Address: St Mary Redcliffe Church
Bristol, BS1 6RA, United Kingdom
Phone: 0117 933 8644

#301
Radford Mill Farm Shop
Cuisines: Tea Room, Deli
Average price: Expensive
Address: 41 Picton Street
Bristol, BS6 5PZ, United Kingdom
Phone: 0117 942 6644

#302
FlavourZ
Cuisines: Buffet, Asian Fusion
Average price: Inexpensive
Address: Colston Avenue
Bristol, BS1 4UB, United Kingdom
Phone: 0117 376 3176

#303
Grounded
Cuisines: Cafe
Average price: Modest
Address: 421-425 Gloucester Road
Bristol, BS7 8TZ, United Kingdom
Phone: 0117 951 1505

#304
The H Bar
Cuisines: Bar, Mediterranean, Spanish
Average price: Modest
Address: Colston Street
Bristol, BS1 5AR, United Kingdom
Phone: 0117 204 7130

#305
Dain Korea
Cuisines: Korean, Asian Fusion
Average price: Modest
Address: 27 Gloucester Rd
Bristol, BS6 5, United Kingdom
Phone: 0117 942 5714

#306
Red Lion
Cuisines: Pub, British
Average price: Modest
Address: 26 Worrall Road
Bristol, BS8 2UE, United Kingdom
Phone: 0117 903 0773

#307
Spice Up Your Life
Cuisines: Indian
Average price: Inexpensive
Address: 7 Exchange Avenue
Bristol, BS1 1JP, United Kingdom
Phone: 0117 914 4448

#308
Eastern Taste
Cuisines: Indian, Fast Food, Bangladeshi
Average price: Inexpensive
Address: 94 St Marks Road
Bristol, BS5 6JH, United Kingdom
Phone: 0117 952 0718

#309
The Albion
Cuisines: Pub, British
Average price: Expensive
Address: Boyces Ave
Bristol, BS8 4AA, United Kingdom
Phone: 0117 973 3522

#310
Krishna's Inn
Cuisines: Indian
Average price: Modest
Address: 4 Byron Place
Bristol, BS8 1JT, United Kingdom
Phone: 0117 927 6864

#311
Slug & Lettuce
Cuisines: Pub, British, Lounge
Average price: Modest
Address: 41 Corn Street
Bristol, BS1 1HT, United Kingdom
Phone: 0117 930 0909

#312
Snuff Mill Harvester
Cuisines: British, Pub
Average price: Expensive
Address: 207 Frenchay Park Road
Bristol, BS16 1LF, United Kingdom
Phone: 0117 956 6560

#313
Coffee#1
Cuisines: Coffee & Tea, Sandwiches
Average price: Modest
Address: 157 Gloucester Road
Bristol, BS7 8BA, United Kingdom
Phone: 0117 942 9909

#314
Prince's Traditional Fish & Chips
Cuisines: Fish & Chips
Average price: Inexpensive
Address: 721 Fishponds Road
Bristol, BS16 3UW, United Kingdom
Phone: 0117 939 9393

#315
Old Lock & Weir
Cuisines: Pub, British
Average price: Modest
Address: Hanham Mills
Bristol, BS15 3NU, United Kingdom
Phone: 0117 967 3793

#316
Boston Tea Party
Cuisines: Coffee & Tea, Sandwiches
Average price: Inexpensive
Address: 1 Princess Victoria Street
Bristol, BS8 4HR, United Kingdom
Phone: 0117 973 4790

#317
Watershed Cafe Bar
Cuisines: Cafe
Average price: Modest
Address: 1 Canons Road
Bristol, BS1 5TX, United Kingdom
Phone: 0117 921 4135

#318
Bedminster Kebab House
Cuisines: Indian
Average price: Inexpensive
Address: 29A East Street
Bristol, BS3 4HH, United Kingdom
Phone: 0117 953 3339

#319
Ali Baba's 40 Dishes
Cuisines: Indian
Average price: Inexpensive
Address: 34 West Street
Bristol, BS3 3LH, United Kingdom
Phone: 0117 966 3713

#320
Natraj Tandoori
Cuisines: Chinese, Himalayan/Nepalese
Average price: Modest
Address: 185 Gloucester Road
Bristol, BS7 8BG, United Kingdom
Phone: 0117 924 8145

#321
Entelia Restaurant
Cuisines: Greek, Mediterranean
Average price: Expensive
Address: 50 Whiteladies Road
Bristol, BS8 2NH, United Kingdom
Phone: 0117 946 6793

#322
Pizza Express
Cuisines: Pizza
Average price: Modest
Address: 35 Corn Street
Bristol, BS1 1HT, United Kingdom
Phone: 0117 930 0239

#323
The Big Bang
Cuisines: British
Average price: Modest
Address: 46 Whiteladies Road
Bristol, BS8 2NH, United Kingdom
Phone: 0117 923 9212

#324
Oriental Chef
Cuisines: Fast Food
Average price: Inexpensive
Address: 64 North Street
Bristol, BS3 1HJ, United Kingdom
Phone: 0117 966 9166

#325
Papadeli Delicatessens
Cuisines: Deli, European
Average price: Expensive
Address: 84 Alma Road
Bristol, BS8 2DJ, United Kingdom
Phone: 0117 973 6569

#326
Starbucks Coffee Company
Cuisines: Coffee & Tea, Cafe
Average price: Expensive
Address: Queens Road
Bristol, BS8 1RE, United Kingdom
Phone: 0117 922 6959

#327
Gala Casinos
Cuisines: Casinos, Nightlife, Steakhouse
Average price: Modest
Address: Explore Lane
Bristol, BS1 5TY, United Kingdom
Phone: 0117 906 9970

#328
Caribbean Soul Food
Cuisines: Caribbean
Average price: Inexpensive
Address: 48 Lynton Road
Bristol, BS3 5LX, United Kingdom
Phone: 07847 297719

#329
Zizzi
Cuisines: Italian
Average price: Modest
Address: 7-8 Triangle South
Bristol, BS8 1EY, United Kingdom
Phone: 0117 929 8700

#330
Oh! Calcutta!
Cuisines: Indian, Pakistani, Fast Food
Average price: Modest
Address: 216-220 Cheltenham Road
Bristol, BS6 5QU, United Kingdom
Phone: 0117 924 0458

#331
Rupsha
Cuisines: Indian
Average price: Modest
Address: 3A Regent Street
Bristol, BS8 4HW, United Kingdom
Phone: 0117 973 9937

#332
Kondi Brasserie
Cuisines: Breakfast & Brunch, Coffee & Tea
Average price: Inexpensive
Address: 105 Henleaze Road
Bristol, BS9 4JP, United Kingdom
Phone: 0117 962 8230

#333
Thali Cafe
Cuisines: Indian
Average price: Modest
Address: North Street
Bristol, BS3 1TF, United Kingdom
Phone: 0117 953 2783

#334
The Pear Cafe
Cuisines: Sandwiches, Coffee & Tea
Average price: Inexpensive
Address: 2 Upper York St
Bristol, BS2 8QN, United Kingdom
Phone: 0117 942 8392

#335
Farrows Fish and Chips
Cuisines: Fast Food, Fish & Chips
Average price: Inexpensive
Address: 146 Wells Road
Bristol, BS4 2AG, United Kingdom
Phone: 0117 908 5511

#336
Bosphorus Restaurant
Cuisines: Turkish
Average price: Modest
Address: 45 Baldwin Street
Bristol, BS1 1RA, United Kingdom
Phone: 0117 922 1333

#337
Fungs Noodle Bar
Cuisines: Chinese
Average price: Inexpensive
Address: 330 Gloucester Road
Bristol, BS7 8TJ, United Kingdom
Phone: 0117 923 2020

#338
The Cambridge Arms
Cuisines: Pub, British
Average price: Modest
Address: Coldharbour Road
Avon BS6 7JS, United Kingdom
Phone: 0117 973 9786

#339
Raj Mahal
Cuisines: Indian, Bangladeshi
Average price: Modest
Address: 8-10 Frome Valley Road
Bristol, BS16 1HD, United Kingdom
Phone: 0117 958 6382

#340
Joe Kebub
Cuisines: Fast Food, Greek, Mediterranean
Average price: Modest
Address: 26 Cannon Street
Bristol, BS3 1BN, United Kingdom
Phone: 0117 904 0019

#341
Snax
Cuisines: Coffee & Tea, Breakfast & Brunch
Average price: Inexpensive
Address: 118 E Street
Bristol, BS3 4EY, United Kingdom
Phone: 0117 953 3957

#342
Dim Sum Oriental Take Away
Cuisines: Fast Food
Average price: Modest
Address: 263 North Street
Bristol, BS3 1JN, United Kingdom
Phone: 0117 953 0606

#343
Ciao
Cuisines: Italian
Average price: Modest
Address: 203 Wellington Hill West
Bristol, BS9 4QL, United Kingdom
Phone: 0117 962 2643

#344
Oz Restaurant
Cuisines: Turkish
Average price: Modest
Address: 3 - 4 Triangle South
Bristol, BS8 1EY, United Kingdom
Phone: 0117 927 3097

#345
Cafe Spice
Cuisines: Indian
Average price: Modest
Address: 154 W Street
Bristol, BS3, United Kingdom
Phone: 0117 953 3623

#346
Happy House
Cuisines: Fast Food
Average price: Inexpensive
Address: 3 Redcatch Road
Bristol, BS4 2EP, United Kingdom
Phone: 0117 977 8709

#347
The Green Man
Cuisines: Pub, British
Average price: Expensive
Address: 21 Alfred Place
Bristol, BS2 8HD, United Kingdom
Phone: 0117 930 4824

#348
Bristol Grill
Cuisines: Fast Food
Average price: Inexpensive
Address: 40 Cannon Street
Bristol, BS3 1BN, United Kingdom
Phone: 0117 966 2694

#349
Caffe Gusto
Cuisines: Coffee & Tea, Sandwiches, Cafe
Average price: Modest
Address: 120 St Michael's Hill
Bristol, BS2 8BU, United Kingdom
Phone: 0117 214 0665

#350
Miss Millie's Fried Chicken
Cuisines: Fast Food
Average price: Inexpensive
Address: 166 Whiteladies Road
Bristol, BS8 2XZ, United Kingdom
Phone: 0117 973 3650

#351
Soho Coffee Co.
Cuisines: Coffee & Tea, Sandwiches
Average price: Inexpensive
Address: Unit SU32 Concorde St
Bristol, BS1 3BF, United Kingdom
Phone: 0117 376 3224

#352
Chans Chow
Cuisines: Fast Food
Average price: Modest
Address: 4A Kellaway Avenue
Bristol, BS6 7XR, United Kingdom
Phone: 0117 923 2868

#353
Allspice
Cuisines: Indian, Fast Food
Average price: Modest
Address: 389 Bath Road
Bristol, BS4 3EU, United Kingdom
Phone: 0117 971 5551

#354
New City Fish Bar
Cuisines: Fish & Chips
Average price: Inexpensive
Address: 378 Filton Avenue
Bristol, BS7 0BE, United Kingdom
Phone: 0117 907 7921

#355
Magic Roll
Cuisines: Sandwiches
Average price: Inexpensive
Address: 9 New Station Rd
Bristol, BS16 3RP, United Kingdom
Phone: 0117 329 4393

#356
Pitcher & Piano
Cuisines: British, Bar
Average price: Modest
Address: Cannon's Road
Bristol, BS1 5UH, United Kingdom
Phone: 0117 929 9652

#357
Antix
Cuisines: British, Lounge
Average price: Modest
Address: 44 Park St
Bristol, BS1 5JG, United Kingdom
Phone: 0117 925 1139

#358
British Raj Lar
Cuisines: Ethiopian, Indian
Average price: Expensive
Address: 1-3 Passage Road
Bristol, BS9 3HN, United Kingdom
Phone: 0117 950 7149

#359
The Mall Deli
Cuisines: Deli
Average price: Modest
Address: 14 The Mall
Bristol, BS8 4, United Kingdom
Phone: 0117 973 4440

#360
Benny's Chicken
Cuisines: Fast Food
Average price: Inexpensive
Address: 15 Gloucester Rd
Bristol, BS7 8AA, United Kingdom
Phone: 0117 924 8588

#361
Good Taste
Cuisines: Malaysian, Chinese, Thai
Average price: Modest
Address: Unit 4 St Annes Village Centre
Bristol, BS4 4WW, United Kingdom
Phone: 0117 971 7170

#362
Biblos
Cuisines: Middle Eastern, Mediterranean
Average price: Inexpensive
Address: 82 Mina Road
Bristol, BS2 9XW, United Kingdom
Phone: 0117 955 8887

#363
Kwans Fish Bar
Cuisines: Fish & Chips
Average price: Inexpensive
Address: 34 North Street
Bristol, BS3 1HW, United Kingdom
Phone: 0117 966 5904

#364
The Clove Indian Restaurant
Cuisines: Indian, Fast Food
Average price: Exclusive
Address: 5 Luckwell Road
Bristol, BS3 3EL, United Kingdom
Phone: 0117 963 9635

#365
La Piazza 1
Cuisines: Italian
Average price: Inexpensive
Address: 777 Fishponds Road
Bristol, BS16, United Kingdom
Phone: 0117 965 0111

#366
Chicken Cottage
Cuisines: British
Average price: Inexpensive
Address: 178 Church Road
Bristol, BS5 9HX, United Kingdom
Phone: 0117 239 9484

#367
The Brass Pig
Cuisines: Bar, British
Average price: Modest
Address: 1 Clifton Heights
Bristol, BS8 1EJ, United Kingdom
Phone: 0117 329 4471

#368
Pinkmans Bakery
Cuisines: Pizza, Coffee & Tea, Bakery
Average price: Modest
Address: 85 Park Street
Bristol, BS1 5PJ, United Kingdom
Phone: 0117 403 2040

#369
Slix
Cuisines: Fast Food, Burgers
Average price: Inexpensive
Address: 89-91 Stokes Croft
Bristol, BS1 3RD, United Kingdom
Phone: 0117 924 8743

#370
Shazz's
Cuisines: Fast Food
Average price: Exclusive
Address: 170 Lawrence Hill
Bristol, BS5 0DN, United Kingdom
Phone: 0117 909 0546

#371
Pizza Casa
Cuisines: Pizza, Fast Food
Average price: Modest
Address: 48 Coldharbour Road
Bristol, BS6 7NA, United Kingdom
Phone: 0117 946 7444

#372
McDonald's
Cuisines: Fast Food, Burgers
Average price: Inexpensive
Address: East Street
Bristol, BS3 4JY, United Kingdom
Phone: 0117 963 1710

#373
Caffe Gusto
Cuisines: Ice Cream, Sandwiches
Average price: Expensive
Address: 9 Princess Victoria Street
Bristol, BS8 4BX, United Kingdom
Phone: 0117 973 5400

#374
Chiquito
Cuisines: Mexican
Average price: Inexpensive
Address: St Philip's Causeway
Bristol, BS2 0SP, United Kingdom
Phone: 0117 972 8292

#375
Wong Tai Sin
Cuisines: Chinese, Fish & Chips, Fast Food
Average price: Inexpensive
Address: 144 Wells Road
Bristol, BS4 2AT, United Kingdom
Phone: 0117 971 9513

#376
Simply Spiced
Cuisines: Fast Food, Indian
Average price: Inexpensive
Address: 88 Mina Road
Bristol, BS2 9XW, United Kingdom
Phone: 0117 955 2419

#377
Baguette Express
Cuisines: Sandwiches, Fast Food
Average price: Inexpensive
Address: 107 East Street
Bristol, BS3 4EX, United Kingdom
Phone: 0117 953 3499

#378
Dragon Grill
Cuisines: Asian Fusion
Average price: Expensive
Address: 1-2 Frogmore St
Bristol, BS1 5NA, United Kingdom
Phone: 0117 929 3288

#379
Brunel Wine Bar
Cuisines: Wine Bar, Tapas Bar
Average price: Modest
Address: 38 The Mall
Bristol, BS8 4DS, United Kingdom
Phone: 0117 973 4443

#380
Pizza Hut
Cuisines: Pizza, Fast Food
Average price: Expensive
Address: 228 Cheltenham Road
Bristol, BS6 5QU, United Kingdom
Phone: 0117 942 2200

#381
Family Kebab House
Cuisines: Fast Food, Steakhouse, Burgers
Average price: Inexpensive
Address: 623 Fishponds Rd
Bristol, BS16 3BA, United Kingdom
Phone: 0117 965 6213

#382
Eastern Tandoori
Cuisines: Fast Food, Indian
Average price: Inexpensive
Address: 81 North Street
Bristol, BS3 1ES, United Kingdom
Phone: 0117 966 2365

#383
George's Restaurant
Cuisines: Cafe
Average price: Inexpensive
Address: 111 East Street
Bristol, BS3 4EX, United Kingdom
Phone: 0117 966 9679

#384
Papa Costa
Cuisines: Deli, Sandwiches
Average price: Inexpensive
Address: 67 Queens Road
Bristol, BS8 1QL, United Kingdom
Phone: 0117 929 1600

#385
Subway
Cuisines: Fast Food, Sandwiches
Average price: Inexpensive
Address: 80-82 East Street
Bristol, BS3 4EY, United Kingdom
Phone: 0117 963 7616

#386
Tgi Fridays
Cuisines: American
Average price: Expensive
Address: Merlin Road
Bristol, BS34 5DG, United Kingdom
Phone: 0117 959 1987

#387
Turmeric
Cuisines: Indian
Average price: Modest
Address: 775 Fishponds Road
Bristol, BS16 3, United Kingdom
Phone: 0117 965 0022

#388
Clark's Pies
Cuisines: Bakery, Deli, Fast Food
Average price: Inexpensive
Address: 259 N Street
Bristol, BS3 1JN, United Kingdom
Phone: 0117 966 3894

#389
The Willy Wicket
Cuisines: Pub, Bistro
Average price: Modest
Address: Badminton Road
Bristol, BS36 1DP, United Kingdom
Phone: 0117 956 7308

#390
Southern Fried Chicken
Cuisines: Fast Food
Average price: Inexpensive
Address: 299 Gloucester Rd
Bristol, BS7 8PE, United Kingdom
Phone: 0117 949 1100

#391
Jade Palace Restaurant
Cuisines: Cafe
Average price: Modest
Address: 277 Two Mile Hill Road
Bristol, BS15 1AX, United Kingdom
Phone: 0117 967 3851

#392
Garam Massala
Cuisines: Indian
Average price: Exclusive
Address: 37 Cotham Hill
Bristol, BS6 6JY, United Kingdom
Phone: 0117 923 7585

#393
Domino's Pizza
Cuisines: Fast Food, Food Delivery Service
Average price: Expensive
Address: 119 Whiteladies Road
Bristol, BS8 2PL, United Kingdom
Phone: 0117 973 3400

#394
Princes Pantry
Cuisines: Fast Food
Average price: Inexpensive
Address: 61 Prince Street
Bristol, BS1 4PH, United Kingdom
Phone: 0117 925 0400

#395
Rendezvous Restaurant
Cuisines: Fish & Chips
Average price: Inexpensive
Address: 9 Denmark Street
Bristol, BS1 5DQ, United Kingdom
Phone: 0117 929 8683

#396
Walkabout
Cuisines: Pub, Sports Bar, British
Average price: Modest
Address: 40 Corn Street
Bristol, BS1 1HQ, United Kingdom
Phone: 0117 930 0181

#397
Lock Keeper
Cuisines: Pub, British
Average price: Modest
Address: Keynsham Road
Bristol, BS31 2DD, United Kingdom
Phone: 0117 986 2383

#398
Henleaze Fish Bar
Cuisines: Fish & Chips
Average price: Modest
Address: 150 Henleaze Road
Bristol, BS9 4NB, United Kingdom
Phone: 0117 907 3383

#399
Portwall Tavern
Cuisines: Pub, British
Average price: Inexpensive
Address: Portwall Lane
Bristol, BS1 6NB, United Kingdom
Phone: 0117 922 0442

#400
Taste of India
Cuisines: Indian
Average price: Inexpensive
Address: 1 Upper Byron Place
Bristol, BS8 1JY, United Kingdom
Phone: 0117 930 0170

#401
Wangs Fish Bar
Cuisines: Fish & Chips, Chinese
Average price: Inexpensive
Address: 200 Wells Rd
Bristol, BS4 2AX, United Kingdom
Phone: 0117 977 6973

#402
Burger King
Cuisines: Fast Food, Burgers
Average price: Inexpensive
Address: St Philips Causeway
Bristol, BS4 3BD, United Kingdom
Phone: 0117 977 0791

#403
Pizza Hut
Cuisines: Pizza, Italian
Average price: Inexpensive
Address: 210 The Mall
Bristol, BS34 5UR, United Kingdom
Phone: 0117 959 2345

#404
Ashyana Indian Cuisine
Cuisines: Indian
Average price: Modest
Address: 238 Henleaze Road
Bristol, BS9 4NG, United Kingdom
Phone: 0117 962 4001

#405
Pizza Express
Cuisines: Pizza
Average price: Modest
Address: 2 Regent Street
Bristol, BS8 4HG, United Kingdom
Phone: 0117 974 4259

#406
Mamma Mia
Cuisines: Italian, Beer, Wine & Spirits
Average price: Modest
Address: 10a Park Row
Bristol, BS1 5LJ, United Kingdom
Phone: 0117 926 8891

#407
Chipping Sodbury Fish Bar
Cuisines: Fish & Chips
Average price: Inexpensive
Address: 53 Broad Street
Bristol, BS37 6AD, United Kingdom
Phone: 01454 313386

#408
Ocean Chinese Fish Bar
Cuisines: Chinese, Fish & Chips
Average price: Inexpensive
Address: 123 Oxford Street
Bristol, BS3 4RH, United Kingdom
Phone: 0117 977 7298

#409
Roll For The Soul
Cuisines: Cafe
Average price: Modest
Address: Quay Street
City Centre BS1 2JL, United Kingdom
Phone: 07596 917946

#410
Huong Que Vietnamese Restaurant
Cuisines: Vietnamese
Average price: Inexpensive
Address: 209 Gloucester Road
Bristol, BS7 8NN, United Kingdom
Phone: 0117 373 8882

#411
Papa John's
Cuisines: Pizza
Average price: Modest
Address: 19 Straits Parade
Bristol, BS16 2LE, United Kingdom
Phone: 0117 965 0808

#412
The Fantastic Sandwich Co
Cuisines: Caterer, Fast Food, Sandwiches
Average price: Inexpensive
Address: 63 North Road
Bristol, BS6 5AD, United Kingdom
Phone: 0117 942 0470

#413
Shadin Indian & Balti Takeaway
Cuisines: Indian
Average price: Modest
Address: 70 Broad Street
Bristol, BS16 5NL, United Kingdom
Phone: 0117 957 5786

#414
Pret A Manger
Cuisines: Coffee & Tea, European
Average price: Inexpensive
Address: 29-30 Queens Road
Bristol, BS8 1QE, United Kingdom
Phone: 0117 945 2304

#415
Pure Pasta, Soup & Sandwich
Cuisines: Italian
Average price: Inexpensive
Address: Unit 30 St Nicholas Market
Bristol, BS1 1LG, United Kingdom
Phone: 07899 862403

#416
Pizza Hut UK
Cuisines: Pizza
Average price: Modest
Address: 703 Fishponds Road
Bristol, BS16 3UH, United Kingdom
Phone: 0117 958 6200

#417
Hotcha
Cuisines: Asian Fusion, Chinese
Average price: Modest
Address: 65 Baldwin Street
Bristol, BS1, United Kingdom
Phone: 0871 288 2282

#418
Mela Indian Takeaway
Cuisines: Fast Food, Indian
Average price: Inexpensive
Address: 19 York Road
Bristol, BS6 5QB, United Kingdom
Phone: 0117 924 9272

#419
Grupo Lounge
Cuisines: Bar, British, Cafe
Average price: Expensive
Address: 8 Canford Lane
Bristol, BS9 3DH, United Kingdom
Phone: 0117 950 0279

#420
Do' Lii Coffee
Cuisines: Coffee & Tea, Breakfast & Brunch
Average price: Modest
Address: 208 Cheltenham Rd
Bristol, BS6 5QU, United Kingdom
Phone: 0117 908 2611

#421
Pizza Hut
Cuisines: Pizza
Average price: Expensive
Address: 23/25 St Augustines Parade
Bristol, BS1 4UL, United Kingdom
Phone: 0117 925 2755

#422
Tinto Lounge
Cuisines: Bar, British, Cafe
Average price: Modest
Address: 344-346 Gloucester Road
Horfield BS7 8TP, United Kingdom
Phone: 0117 942 0526

#423
Parsons Bakery
Cuisines: Bakery, Fast Food
Average price: Modest
Address: 252 North St
Bristol, BS3 1JA, United Kingdom
Phone: 0117 963 9000

#424
Charcoal Grill
Cuisines: Fast Food
Average price: Inexpensive
Address: 3 Broad Walk
Bristol, BS4 2RA, United Kingdom
Phone: 0117 300 9994

#425
Old Cheese Shop
Cuisines: Sandwiches
Average price: Inexpensive
Address: 1 Worrall Road
Bristol, BS8 2UF, United Kingdom
Phone: 0117 946 6940

#426
Quick Crepes
Cuisines: Creperie, Desserts, Coffee & Tea
Average price: Inexpensive
Address: City Centre
Bristol, BS1, United Kingdom
Phone: 01225 783050

#427
Bombay Boulevard
Cuisines: Indian
Average price: Inexpensive
Address: 4 Denmark St
Bristol, BS1 5DQ, United Kingdom
Phone: 0117 927 3544

#428
Pumpkin Cafe
Cuisines: Coffee & Tea, Cafe
Average price: Modest
Address: Temple Meads Train Station
Bristol, BS1 6QG, United Kingdom
Phone: 0117 925 2953

#429
Quba Ice
Cuisines: Caribbean
Average price: Modest
Address: 220 North Street
Bristol, BS3 1JD, United Kingdom
Phone: 0117 963 9222

#430
Wok Inn
Cuisines: Chinese
Average price: Modest
Address: 758 Fishponds Road
Bristol, BS16 3UA, United Kingdom
Phone: 0117 965 8882

#431
Made Up
Cuisines: Fast Food
Average price: Modest
Address: 49a Whiteladies Road
Bristol, BS8 2LS, United Kingdom
Phone: 0845 463 5352

#432
Lashings Coffee House
Cuisines: Cafe
Average price: Inexpensive
Address: 7 Lower Redland Road
Bristol, BS6 6TB, United Kingdom
Phone: 0117 973 7059

#433
Evolution
Cuisines: Cafe, Dance Club
Average price: Modest
Address: U Shed Canons Road
Bristol, BS1 5UH, United Kingdom
Phone: 0117 922 0330

#434
China Capital
Cuisines: Thai, Malaysian, Chinese
Average price: Inexpensive
Address: 24 Ashton Road
Bristol, BS3 2EA, United Kingdom
Phone: 0117 953 9666

#435
Lick'N Chick'N
Cuisines: Fast Food
Average price: Inexpensive
Address: 452 Stapleton Road
Bristol, BS5 6PA, United Kingdom
Phone: 0117 951 1000

#436
Mumtaz Restaurant
Cuisines: Indian, Pakistani
Average price: Modest
Address: 61 High Street
Bristol, BS9 3ED, United Kingdom
Phone: 0117 950 7771

#437
Jessica's Sandwich Bar
Cuisines: Coffee & Tea, Cafe
Average price: Inexpensive
Address: 176 Kings Head Lane
Bristol, BS13 7BW, United Kingdom
Phone: 0117 946 5919

#438
The Crown Inn Harvester
Cuisines: British, Pub
Average price: Modest
Address: 126 Bath Road
Bristol, BS30 9DE, United Kingdom
Phone: 0117 932 2846

#439
Bella Italia
Cuisines: Italian
Average price: Inexpensive
Address: 8-10 Baldwin Street
Bristol, BS1 1SA, United Kingdom
Phone: 0117 929 3278

#440
Havana Coffee Clifton Village
Cuisines: Cafe
Average price: Modest
Address: 6 Clifton Down Rd
Bristol, BS8 4AD, United Kingdom
Phone: 0117 329 0212

#441
Posh Spice
Cuisines: Indian, Pakistani
Average price: Modest
Address: 86 High Street
Bristol, BS48 1AS, United Kingdom
Phone: 01275 854560

#442
Beijing Express
Cuisines: Fast Food
Average price: Modest
Address: 230 ST. Johns Lane
Bristol, BS3 5AU, United Kingdom
Phone: 0117 963 9888

#443
McDonald's
Cuisines: American, Fast Food
Average price: Inexpensive
Address: Sheene Road
Bristol, BS3 4EG, United Kingdom
Phone: 0117 953 3755

#444
Noa
Cuisines: Japanese
Average price: Expensive
Address: 12 - 13 Waterloo St
Bristol, BS8 4BT, United Kingdom
Phone: 0117 973 2881

#445
Mr Crispins
Cuisines: Fish & Chips
Average price: Inexpensive
Address: 280 Wells Road
Bristol, BS4 2PU, United Kingdom
Phone: 0117 987 9333

#446
Domus Pizza
Cuisines: Pizza, Fast Food
Average price: Inexpensive
Address: 183 Whiteladies Road
Bristol, BS8 2RY, United Kingdom
Phone: 0117 946 6100

#447
McDonald's
Cuisines: Burgers
Average price: Inexpensive
Address: 24-26 Merchant Street
Bristol, BS1 3EP, United Kingdom
Phone: 0117 927 2417

#448
Easton Express
Cuisines: Japanese, Chinese
Average price: Inexpensive
Address: 186 Stapleton Rd
Bristol, BS5 0NZ, United Kingdom
Phone: 0117 951 2267

#449
Perfect Pizza
Cuisines: Pizza, Italian
Average price: Modest
Address: 13 Straits Parade
Bristol, BS16 2LE, United Kingdom
Phone: 0117 958 4848

#450
New Hong Kong Fish Bar
Cuisines: Fast Food
Average price: Inexpensive
Address: 186 Bedminster Down Road
Bristol, BS13 7AF, United Kingdom
Phone: 0117 966 8030

23657307R00024

Printed in Great Britain
by Amazon